The RAF Battle of Britain Memorial Flight Avro Lancaster, City of Lincoln, just before landing at RAF Coningsby.

Designed by Dan Patterson. Edited by Katherine A. Neale and Ross A. Howell, Jr.

Library of Congress Catalog Card Number 96-75272

ISBN 1-57427-052-4

Printed in Hong Kong

Published by Howell Press, Inc. 1147 River Road, Suite 2, Charlottesville, VA 22901 Telephone 804-977-4006

First printing

HOWELL PRESS

Previous page: A collection of personal and service items from the RAF. At top left, over the fleece "Irvin" jacket, a strip of "Window," the foil released in large quantities to confuse German radar. Top right is the battle dress uniform inside a "Sidcott" flight suit, a British "Mae West" inflatable life preserver, and a standard British parachute. To the left of the parachute are the leather gauntlets necessary for high-altitude flying. Further left is an RAF service cap, a British "G" oxygen mask, and a "C" leather flying helmet.

Looking to the eight o'clock position from the mid-upper turret, beyond the vertical stabilizer, the Battle of Britain Memorial Flight's Hawker Hurricane.

Preface

Before I began this book, I tried to read and learn as much as possible about the Lancaster and RAF Bomber Command. I read all the technical and historical information I could get my hands on about these great bombers and their crews. I attempted to absorb the staggering numbers that represent the losses that the bomber force had taken during World War II.

As an American, I can never understand what it was like to be under the bombs of an enemy in my home, to have been *the target* of those bombs or to have some nameless aviator try to kill me or my family. I actually had to be there before I could begin to understand the enormous price paid by the men and women of Britain and her allies in maintaining their massive air assault against Germany.

My first trip to the UK was to make the photos for this book. I was struck by the memorials in every village, from "the first war" as well as World War II. Author Ron Dick and I were there during the VJ Day celebrations, and I saw everywhere the display of pride and remembrance, veterans of the war proudly wearing their decorations, men and women.

We talked to a veteran of the bomber offensive, a Lancaster crewman, named Ron Emeny. He was shot down before the D-Day invasion, in a force of Lancasters that started out as 92 bombers . . . 45 were shot down. Mr. Emeny, badly burned as he bailed out, was picked up by the French and nursed back to health. He proudly wore the gold pin of "The Caterpillar Club" awarded to those who "hit the silk" and returned. He fought with the Resistance before escaping over the Pyrenees and coming back to England. He killed several German soldiers and to this day doesn't regret getting back at those who had brought so much grief to him and his country. He said that in a little church in France, there are 11 flower pots hanging from the ceiling. Those flower pots are German helmets suspended upside down, now filled with flowers. They are the helmets of men he killed one night.

As an American, I can only try to understand what it was like to be *the target* of an enemy and to have the opportunity to strike back.

Dan Patterson
February 4, 1996

LANCASTER

RAF Heavy Bomber

Photographs by Dan Patterson
Text by Air Vice-Marshal Ron Dick

THE LANCASTER

Air Power Theory and Reality between the Wars

By the time Nazi Germany was bludgeoned to defeat in 1945, Bomber Command of the Royal Air Force had evolved into an awesome instrument of destruction. Its capacity to wreak havoc on an opposing nation was formidable, and there was no doubt that its aircrews and their aircraft had played a significant part in bringing the Third Reich to its knees. Bomber Command's principal weapon for the assault was the Lancaster, an aircraft of which inter-war air power theorists must have dreamed. In 1945, the Lancaster, with its huge bomb bay and its acquired array of electronic devices, was indeed a bomber to be feared, but the path to its development had been long and painful, marked as it was by both political struggle and lack of military understanding.

Lancaster prototype.

Imperial War Museum

"Oh boy, oh boy! What an aeroplane!"
Roy Dobson, Managing Director, Avro

In the years following its formation as an independent service in 1918, the Royal Air Force was compelled to fight off a number of fierce challenges to its continued existence. Parsimonious post-WWI budgets forced painful cuts in the British armed services and powerful arguments were made, particularly by the army and the navy, in attempts to show that a separate RAF was an unjustifiable extravagance. To preserve its hard-won independence, the RAF needed a doctrine to emphasize the use of air power in roles beyond the competence of the other two services. The most significant element of that doctrine grew out of the strategic air power theories vigorously promoted by the RAF's Chief of Air Staff, Sir Hugh Trenchard. He firmly believed that the air force's principal role should involve leaping over intervening armies and navies to rain devastating blows on an enemy's heartland. In his view, those blows would be directed not only at military and industrial targets, but also at an enemy nation's civil population, thereby undermining national morale.

It was one thing to found a doctrine based on strategic air power theory, but it was quite another to provide the means with which to carry it out. Between the world wars the RAF lived and grew under the mantle of the Trenchard doctrine, but a blind eye was turned to the fact that neither the aircrew training system nor the available bombers were capable of meeting its demands. "Devastating blows" delivered by aircraft like the Vickers Virginia and the Handley Page Heyford (the last of the "cloth bomber" biplanes) would have been no more than pinpricks to an industrial nation. Even the newer twin-engine monoplane bombers of the 1930s — the Hampden, Whitley, and Wellington — were only transitional. They proved to be sadly inadequate for the strategic task when tested in the crucible of war.

Fortunately for the RAF, some members of the Air Plans staff in the 1930s had taken note of developments elsewhere, notably in Germany and the United States, and had begun to think realistically about strategic bombers and their capabilities. In 1936, the Air Ministry issued specifications for a new class of heavy bombers, aircraft which would have the range and carrying capacity to match the strategic requirement. These gave rise in 1940 to the four-engine Short Stirling and Handley Page Halifax, and the twin-engine Avro Manchester. The Manchester was a huge disap-

pointment, a failure largely because of its temperamental Rolls-Royce Vulture engines, but from the ashes of its failure rose its incomparable offspring — the Lancaster. With longer wings and four Rolls-Royce Merlins, the unloved Manchester was transformed into an aircraft which looked right and was right, a bomber which came to be revered by its crews and feared by the German people as the scourge of their cities.

The Lancaster

The first flight of the Lancaster prototype (serial BT308, then still referred to as the Manchester III) took place on January 9, 1941. It was impressive from the start. As it lifted off the runway at Ringway airport, Avro's managing director, Roy Dobson, turned to his chief designer, Roy Chadwick, and burst out: "Oh boy, oh boy! What an aeroplane!" His initial enthusiasm was to be fully justified. Compared to other wartime aircraft, the Lancaster went through its trials and its service life needing very little fundamental modification. At the same time, its design was such that incorporating minor modifications or fitting new equipment was always relatively easy. What was more, it soon became apparent that Roy Chadwick had conceived an aircraft which was noticeably more capable than the contempo-

Lancaster Mark IIIs of Number 619 Squadron.

after only 300 were completed. The Mk III was essentially the same as the Mk I, the basic difference being that it was fitted with Packard-built Merlins. Three thousand thirty-nine Mk IIIs were built. Taken together with a small number of little known variants such as the Mks VI and VII, which appeared towards the end of the war, the total Lancaster production was 7,377. A few were modified to Mk I (Special) configuration to allow for the carriage of specially shaped or very large weapons, such as the massive 22,000-pound "Grand Slam" bomb and the cylindrical "bouncing bomb" used against German dams. When carrying something as large as the "Grand Slam," the Lancaster was without nose, dorsal, or ventral turrets, and had the bomb doors replaced by a fairing which only partially shielded the bomb.

The Lancaster was regarded with affection by its crews not only because it was generally superior to its bomber rivals, but also because it was an aircraft with few vices. To quote one ecstatic pilot: ". . . the Lanc was something else. It didn't fly; it soared!" It was rugged enough to survive considerable battle damage, and it still flew quite well after the loss of two engines. Although the controls were relatively heavy, the Lancaster was a lively performer and could be thrown around with some violence in the "corkscrew" evasive maneuver, a disorienting sequence of steep wingovers, rapid descents, and high-G pull-outs. Flown with determination, a "corkscrew" was a challenging test of both aircraft and crew, but many Lancaster crews came back to attest to its effectiveness in shaking off attacks by Luftwaffe night fighters.

The Lancaster was noticeably better than its rivals when it came to surviving the hazards of battle and coming home, but it was not so good for the crews once it had been caught by the defenses and shot down. Only two parachute exits were listed in the pilot's notes. One, in the floor of the bomb aimer's compartment in the nose, was recommended for use by all aircrew "if time is available." It was, of course, as far from many of them as it was possible to get, and almost unreachable if the aircraft was under high G-loading. The other was the main fuselage door, which might have been better but for the warning that it

rary and superficially similar Halifax. (One pilot who flew both types went so far as to say about the Halifax: "Compared with the Lanc it looked like a designer's mistake from the outside and was built like one on the inside. We often wondered whether Hitler had had a hand in the design.")

The first production Lancaster I (L7527) flew for the first time on October 31, 1941, powered by four Merlin XX engines, each delivering 1,390 horsepower at takeoff. Its performance was so outstanding that large-scale production was soon authorized, both at Avro and at a number of other factories in the aircraft and automobile industries. By the time its operational service began, the maximum takeoff weight of the standard Lancaster I had risen to 63,000 pounds. It boasted four gun turrets — nose, tail, dorsal, and ventral—and these might have provided impressive defensive cover had it been possible to arm them with heavier weapons than .303-caliber Brownings. Six main fuel tanks gave a total capacity of 2,154 Imperial gallons, which allowed a still air range with a full bomb bay of 1,660 miles when cruising at 210 MPH and 20,000 feet.

As with any new aircraft, the Lancaster was not entirely free of shortcomings or teeth-

ing troubles. Early structural defects were revealed in the wing tips and the tail assembly and a few aircraft were lost due to structural failure before the faults were corrected. A number of difficulties were also experienced initially with the fuel system, but these were quickly put right. Less amenable to rapid correction were the inherent operational weaknesses of an aircraft which, in 1942, was ill-equipped to defend itself against enemy fighters or to find and hit its targets accurately by night. The problems of effective self-defense armament were never adequately dealt with, although some Lancasters were fitted with .50-caliber Brownings in the tail when these weapons became more readily available later in the war. Navigation and bombing did improve markedly, however, as new equipment was fitted and better techniques were developed, and by 1945 the Lancaster force was capable of obliterating any target it was aimed at.

There were three main production variants of the Lancaster. The Mk I predominated, with 3,425 being built. The Mk II was designed as an insurance policy to guard against the possibility of a Merlin engine shortage. Powered by four Bristol Hercules radials, its performance never quite matched that of its Merlin-powered cousins and production ceased should be used "only in extreme emergency" because of the likelihood that anyone leaving that way would strike the tail. Other hatches provided in the roof (for instance, over the pilot's head) were very small and were described only as "crash exits." As a result, only a little over ten percent of Lancaster aircrew survived the destruction of their aircraft, compared to the overall Command figure of about 20 percent.

Standard bomb load.   Imperial War Museum

The heart of the Lancaster was its exceptionally capacious bomb bay. This huge, uninterrupted, rectangular cavern in the aircraft's belly was the reason why the Lancaster was capable of carrying a larger bomb than any other wartime aircraft. Until the much later appearance of Boeing's B-29, an aircraft almost twice the Lancaster's size, no other wartime aircraft could approach the Lancaster in total bomb-carrying capacity, and it was the only bomber to drop the "Grand Slam." A "standard" load for a Lancaster was 12,000 pounds, usually combining a single 4,000-pound "Blockbuster" and an assortment of 1,000-pound,

500-pound, or 250-pound bombs, together with a number of 250-pound containers carrying incendiaries.

A study completed as early as 1943 noted that 132 tons of bombs were dropped for each Lancaster lost on operations. This compared very favorably with tonnages for the Halifax and Stirling, which were 56 and 41 respectively. By the end of the war, Lancasters had flown more than 156,000 operational sorties and dropped more than 608,000 tons of bombs. (As a comparison, the B-17s and B-24s of the 8th Air Force together flew some 295,000 sorties in dropping 641,000 tons.)

Early Efforts

The first unit to be equipped with the Lancaster was Number 44 Squadron at RAF Waddington in December 1941, followed by Number 97 Squadron at RAF Coningsby in January 1942. Number 44 Squadron began the Lancaster's operational record with some modest mine-laying in the Heligoland Bight on March 3, 1942, and then sent two aircraft with the bomber force against Essen a week later. Number 44 Squadron also had the doubtful distinction of suffering the first Lancaster loss in combat, during a mine-laying operation off the French coast on March 24, 1942.

This relatively quiet settling-in period ended on April 17, when Air Marshal Sir Arthur Harris, Commander-in-Chief, Bomber Command, introduced a startling change of pace by launching a daring raid against the M.A.N. submarine diesel engine factory at Augsburg in southern Germany, a target 500 miles deep in enemy territory. Twelve Lancasters, six each from Numbers 44 and 97 Squadrons, flew at low-level in daylight to carry out the attack. The bombing of those which reached the target was accurate and some damage was done to the factory, but the cost was horrifying. Seven of the twelve aircraft were shot down, four by fighters on the way to Augsburg and the others by flak in the target area. All of the returning Lancasters were heavily damaged by flak. The sole survivor of the 44 Squadron contingent was the raid leader, Sqn Ldr J.D. Nettleton, who was awarded the Victoria Cross.

Despite the forbidding example of Augsburg, the experiment of conducting daylight low-level operations with unescorted heavy bombers was repeated six months later when 94 Lancasters attacked the Le Creusot armament works in France. This time evasive routing over the Bay of Biscay helped in achieving complete surprise. The force was not intercepted and the only loss occurred when a Lancaster of Number 61 Squadron bombed Le Creusot power station at such a low level that it struck a building.

That the force had indeed been flying at very low altitudes was confirmed by the post-raid remarks of one crew member who reported that the railway lines in France looked rusty, and another who thought the cows were underfed.

Re-equipping the Force

Behind rare headline-grabbing attacks like those on Augsburg and Le Creusot, the Lancaster force was steadily built up and introduced to the nightly grind of Bomber Command operations. The squadrons of the Command's Number 5 Group were the first to be completely re-equipped, bidding thankful farewells to their hazardous Manchesters and aging Hampdens. Seventy-three 5 Group Lancasters were included in the RAF's first thousand-bomber raid on Cologne on May 30, 1942. By the end of the year, 5 Group alone could lift a heavier bomb load than could the whole of Bomber Command before the Lancaster's arrival. As time went by and the trickle of Lancasters became a flood, the type gained overwhelming predominance in Bomber Command, and at the end of the war it was being operated by no less than 56 frontline bomber squadrons. On March 21, 1945, the Command's records showed 745 Lancasters ready for operations and a further 296 available from the operational conversion units.

When it first appeared, the Lancaster, admirable though it was as an aircraft, suffered from the same limitations as its predecessors when it came to using its potential effectively. However, in 1942 things began to change as new aids to bombing and navigation promised great improvements in operational performance. First on the scene was "Gee," a navigation aid which depended on radio pulses transmitted from several beacons in the UK. Using a cathode ray tube and special plotting charts, a navigator could track the position of his aircraft with reasonable accuracy out to 350 miles or so. "Gee" coverage was therefore effectively limited to western Germany, but that included targets in the Ruhr and such northern cities as Hamburg. While "Gee" was not good enough to be a bombing aid, since its margin of error was measured in miles, in 1942 it could at least provide assurance that an aircraft was in the target area. German jamming soon degraded even that advantage, but "Gee" always remained an important aid for aircraft returning to base.

Close behind "Gee" came "Oboe," which relied on the transmission of radar pulses audible to the pilot and, with a margin of error in hundreds of yards, was accurate enough to be a bombing aid. Once again, it was a device which relied on "line of sight" transmission and therefore had limited range. "H2S," however, was quite different. It was the world's first airborne ground-mapping radar and did not need external transmissions. Later came "GH," a system which overcame many of the limitations of "Gee" and "Oboe," and which allowed aircraft to bomb through cloud cover with impressive accuracy. In parallel with these technological advances came new techniques. In an effort to swamp the defenses, the practice of dispersing the force over several targets each night was ended, and the bombers were formed into streams concentrated in time and space. "Pathfinder" units were formed to find and mark the targets for the main force with flares of varied color, and "Master Bombers" were introduced who stayed over the target to orchestrate the attack.

Other advances included a simple jammer which broadcast Merlin engine noise over German fighter control frequencies, a tail warning radar to detect night fighters, an improved bombsight, target illumination flares which were hooded to avoid blinding bomb aimers,

Lancaster Mark IIIs of Number 106 Squadron.

and "Window" — metallic foil strips which saturated enemy radars. All of these devices undoubtedly contributed to the forging of Bomber Command into the fearsome offensive weapon that it became, but some of them did so at a price. It appeared to take some time for the Command to realize that the new electronic wonders turned any aircraft which used them into powerful homing beacons, and that the Luftwaffe was only too pleased to make use of them for its night fighters.

Normal Operations

During the daylight hours before a night raid, while the bomber crews did their best to relax, the rest of the base bustled with activity. Once the target for the night was known, briefings were prepared on routes to be flown, the size and timing of the raid, the target, enemy defenses, the weather, signals procedures, and "friendly" activities such as target marking and diversionary raids. The parachute section got busy on the aircrew's emergency equipment, and the bomb dump began assembling the weapons loads. In the cookhouse, coffee was poured into thermos flasks, and the knives were out, cutting sandwiches.

Out at the aircraft dispersals, each Lancaster had its engines and systems thoroughly checked, a job which could be a considerable challenge on a bleak winter's day. An engine fitter on Number 467 Squadron, describing a typical scene in 1943, said: "[Our Lancaster] stood completely covered in white hoar frost; from each airscrew hung a two-inch wide icicle leading to the ground, and tapes holding engine and turret covers were frozen solid." Working with bare hands on metal in those conditions — changing plugs, cleaning filters, refueling, and so on — was something of an ordeal. While all this was going on, the armorers tested turrets and guns and loaded ammunition, with nearly twice as much ammunition going to the tail turret as to the other turrets put together. Those Lancasters needing more than routine servicing, or which were just back from major overhaul or repair, were air tested before being bombed-up.

Eventually, the nerve-stretching period of waiting for the aircrews was broken by the preflight briefings. A typical Lancaster base was home to two squadrons, each of which would normally be required to provide 20 aircraft for a raid. Briefing therefore involved some 280 aircrew. By the time it came, they already had some idea of the sort of operation it would be because they had discovered the fuel and bombloads being handled by the ground crews. Nervous tension had been building for hours, relieved only temporarily by the banter between crew members at the preflight meal, usually of such wartime luxuries as bacon and eggs.

With the introduction of the Lancaster and the other four-engine types, briefings in Bomber Command took on a formal and standardized air. First, there were briefings to individual aircrew specialists — navigators, wireless operators, etc. — before everyone gathered together for the main event. The CO drew back the curtains on the wall map to reveal the route and the target, and then the "met" man, the intelligence officer, and the various specialist leaders went through the essentials of the operation, emphasizing such things as the need to avoid bombing "creep-back" and the importance of dropping "Window" at precise intervals. The CO ended the proceedings by wishing everyone luck, and then the aircrew went off to get changed into flying clothing, collect parachutes and "Mae West" life jackets, and clear their pockets of all personal possessions. More than a few went through fixed rituals as they got ready, dressing in a particular way or gathering up lucky mascots. Then they climbed into the transport and were driven to their waiting aircraft.

Out at the dispersals there was always some spare time to be spent talking to the ground crew or just lying about, smoking. For many aircrew, this was the worst part of the whole day, a period when all was ready but it was not yet time to go. The quietness of the open airfield was in stark contrast to what was to come, and they had no choice but to confront their fears.

At last the moment came when the aircrew climbed the short ladder at the rear of the Lancaster's slab-sided fuselage, incarcerat-ing themselves in the gloom of its functional interior for the next several hours. It stank of the fluids needed by a military aircraft — aviation fuel, engine oil, hydraulic fluid, and most of all, kerosene, used by the ground crew as a universal cleaning liquid. Each man struggled into the confinements of his allotted space, those towards the front of the aircraft having to negotiate the hurdles of the massive wing spars running through the center of the fuselage.

The normal crew for a Lancaster was seven men — pilot, navigator, bomb aimer, flight engineer, wireless operator, mid-upper gunner, and tail gunner. (The ventral turret originally provided was replaced in most Lancasters by the "H2S" radar scanner and its dome.) An early decision had been made to configure the RAF's heavy bombers for just one pilot, largely because it was not thought that the flying training schools could cope with the increased demand if there were two. An essential element of the Lancaster's design, therefore, was "George," the automatic pilot.

In the Lancaster, the pilot sat high up on the left-hand side of the cockpit, with a splendid field of view all round. He was the only member of the crew with any built-in protection, a single sheet of armor plate fitted behind his back. Whatever his rank, he was the aircraft captain. Many sergeant pilots flew with commissioned navigators, but this was not a source of friction. In the air, all pilots were "the skipper," and in controlling the aircraft, they coordinated the efforts of the crew. The outstanding Lancaster captains — men like Guy Gibson, Leonard Cheshire, Micky Martin, and Bill Reid — were natural leaders, but they were often regarded as being lucky, too. The truth was that they made their own luck by working hard and leaving nothing to chance. They knew their aircraft thoroughly and could fly it to the limits, particularly during evasive action, and in transit to and from the target neither they nor their aircraft were still for long. They moved their heads constantly to eliminate canopy blind spots, and banked every few moments to let the gunners search under the aircraft. Like most careful captains, they checked on their crews regularly over the intercom throughout the trip. Micky Martin made a point of insisting that his crew check every detail of their aircraft far more meticulously than was strictly required. He personally polished every square inch of his cockpit canopy to remove the smallest smear, and he taxied to the firing range to let his gunners realign their guns before each trip. On the occasions when luck may have played a part in his survival, Micky Martin had earned it.

The only man further forward than the pilot was the bomb aimer, who occupied a position in the nose. From there he reported on landmarks for the navigator, manned the nose turret guns (seldom used because Luftwaffe pilots were understandably reluctant to attack from head-on at night), managed the deployment of "Window" with the flight engineer, and delivered the bombs. After bomb release, a downward-facing camera took a flash photograph of the area bombed.

Immediately behind the pilot and to his right was the flight engineer. He looked after the engines and systems, managed the fuel, and attempted running repairs when needed. A fold-down seat beside the pilot allowed him to be positioned to assist as necessary with throttle and pitch controls, flaps, undercarriage, and, in an emergency, with propeller feathering and the engine fire extinguishers. Flight engineers were generally given a certain amount of flight instruction to enable them at least to fly the aircraft straight and level if the pilot was incapacitated.

Further back was the navigator, sitting sideways at a small plotting table to the rear of

Lancaster Mark I being refueled at RAF Waddington.

the pilot's seat. He was probably the most heavily occupied member of the crew throughout a trip, engaged as he was in taking frequent fixes, keeping the flight log, and giving adjustments of course and speed to the pilot. The navigator's compartment was the only crew position in the aircraft which was lit, and it was therefore curtained off. Engrossed in his work and shut away in a private world behind his curtains, a navigator could often make himself almost oblivious to the dangers of the night around him.

Just behind the navigator, opposite the wing's leading edge, came the wireless operator, facing a wall of radio and other equipment. Although operations were always flown under radio silence, he was kept busy monitoring his Group frequency, listening for enemy radio traffic, and operating the jammers and tail warning radar.

The gunners were physically the most isolated members of the crew, and their job was as demanding as any. Most of the time, gunners sat in their icy turrets staring into the darkness and seeing nothing. Maintaining a sharp edge while doing this for several hours at a stretch was a considerable challenge, and beyond the capacities of most. Yet the survival of the aircraft frequently depended on their vigilance and the speed with which they reacted to the hint of a fighter (or another bomber) against the blackness of the sky. To counter their problems, gunners took caffeine tablets to stay awake, smeared lanolin on their necks to ease the chafing of constantly turning heads, and tried to protect their night vision by never looking at the flames of a burning target. Many improved their chances by accepting an intensification of the bitter cold, removing the center square of Perspex from their turret to leave a clear space through which there was no possibility of distortion or reflection.

With everyone in place and ready for the preflight checks, it was time to start engines. Normally the starboard inner engine would be started first, because it supplied power for all the main services — hydraulics, pneumatics, and electrics. With the ground crew's battery cart (the "trolley acc") plugged in, and the ground/flight switch set to ground, the

pilot went through the engine start sequence — master fuel cocks off, throttles open half an inch, props fully fine, slow-running switches to idle cutoff, supercharger in M gear, air intake cold, radiator shutters automatic, fuel selector to Number 2 tank, and booster pump on. Then it was thumbs up out of the pilot's window, ignition and booster coil on, and starter button pressed. The propeller began to turn, slowly. At this stage, one lucky ground crew member would be hanging on halfway up the undercarriage leg where, as the Lancaster Pilots' Notes say, he would: ". . . work the priming pump (situated in the wheel well) as

Wireless operator at his station.

firmly as possible while the engine is being turned." On a cold winter's day, that might mean 12 strokes of the priming pump, and it was necessary to continue priming in the ensuing propeller blast until the engine was running smoothly.

The airfield's evening quiet was shattered by the throaty voice of the first Merlin— a preliminary cough, a few bangs, and then a surge into a steady roar. At other dispersals, more Merlins joined in, until the airfield was swallowed up by the sound of more than a hundred powerful piston engines. The sound swelled and faded as they warmed up, first at 1,500 RPM to test magnetos, and then at full power to check takeoff boost and RPM. With after start procedures complete, hydraulics tested by operating the flaps, instruments checked,

and aircraft acceptance forms signed, the pilot waved chocks away, opening the throttles in a burst of power to get his 35-ton monster moving forward. On the intercom, each crew member checked in and confirmed that his oxygen was flowing. The Lancaster moved slowly along the taxiway, joining a long line of similar dark shapes rumbling to the end of the runway.

Before takeoff they ran through the final checks — auto pilot clutch in, DR compass set, pitot heat on, trims set, props fully fine, mixture rich, fuel system checked, super-chargers in M gear, air intakes cold, radiators automatic, and flaps 15 degrees. On a green light from the runway controller, the pilot lined up and opened the throttles, leading slightly with the port outer to counter a tendency to swing to the left. (The Lancaster II, with radial engines, went the other way.) At full power (usually +9 inches boost and 3,000 RPM), with all four Merlins in full song and every rivet in the Lanc vibrating, most pilots

---

It was the opinion of at least one Lancaster engine fitter that "Those who have never climbed up the wheel of a Lanc to reach the engine priming positions have missed out on life!"

Lancaster Mark III of Number IX Squadron takes off.

Imperial War Museum

handed over the throttles to the flight engineer before easing forward on the control column, aiming to raise the tail as soon as possible. Carrying a full load, the Lancaster seemed to roll forever, but finally, the wings flexing madly upward to take the weight, it lumbered into the air at 105 MPH or so. The wheels came up immediately, with the flaps following at 500 feet, after which the aircraft was settled at a climbing speed between 155 and 175 MPH.

As the number of aircraft available to Bomber Command rose, so did the hazards of night operations. Climbing out and forming into a stream could be a worrying time for a crew, particularly since large numbers of other bombers were similarly engaged, unseen in the darkness but occasionally felt as their slipstreams made an aircraft buck and rear. A 101 Squadron captain, flying a Lancaster known as *Gremlin Queen*, was badly shaken by a near collision at 18,000 feet on the night of March 9, 1943: "I had just turned the aircraft on course and, looking up, saw approaching at great speed what appeared to be red balls of fire. . . . I realized after a little hesitation that I was looking down the flame traps of the exhausts of another aircraft approaching head-on, and immediately commenced a turn to starboard. My port wing had barely lifted when the other

aircraft passed us; it was so close we actually heard its engines." Other crews were not so fortunate. Collision was an ever-present hazard on any mission, even though the actual number of aircraft lost in this way was surprisingly small. Perhaps the most celebrated example came on May 30, 1942, during the first thousand-bomber raid on Cologne. At briefing, the crews were reassured about the risk of collision, being told that the statisticians had calculated that only two of the more than 1,000 aircraft would collide during the raid. At one base, a plaintive voice from among the aircrew called out: "Have the boffins worked out which two aircraft it will be?" (It turned out that the statisticians were right. Two aircraft did indeed collide over Cologne, including the one Lancaster lost that night.)

For most raids, Lancasters operated from between 20,000 and 22,000 feet, and they made every effort to be at that altitude before crossing into enemy airspace. In the early days of "H2S" radar, it would be used to give an accurate point of departure from the English coast. Later it was realized that the Germans could watch raids building up by detecting "H2S" transmissions and it was ordered that the radar should not be switched on until the enemy coast was crossed, and even

then used with restraint. Established on course and at his cruising altitude, the pilot throttled back to maintain 160 MPH indicated airspeed (about 215 MPH true airspeed at 20,000 feet). Most of the crew then concentrated on keeping a good lookout, straining their eyes into the night to watch for other bombers and, later, for enemy fighters. Chattering among the crew was discouraged. There were times when split seconds could mean the difference between life and death, and it was not a good idea to have the intercom cluttered up with small talk when a fighter arrived and evasive action was called for. Generally the only break in the droning monotony of the outbound flight was when the gunners asked for permission to clear their guns, and the clatter of Brownings briefly shook the aircraft.

As the enemy coast was approached, "Windowing" was begun, usually handled by the flight engineer, who stuffed a bundle out of a chute in the nose every two minutes. This effectively covered German radar screens in "snow" and denied the enemy precise information about the raid. It was first used on the night of July 24, 1943, during the first raid of the Battle of Hamburg, and it rendered the defenses virtually useless. "Window" blanketed the radars controlling both fighters and flak guns, and blinded the "Lichtenstein" airborne radars of the night fighters. Seven hundred twenty-eight aircraft, 347 of them Lancasters, dropped 2,284 tons of bombs on Hamburg in just 50 minutes. Before July 24, 1943, losses during major raids had been averaging between four and six percent of the force, but "Window" so confused the defenses for Hamburg on this night that only 12 bombers were shot down, four of them Lancasters, for a loss rate of 1.5 percent.

The first Hamburg raid was followed up by the RAF on the nights of July 27, July 29, and August 2, 1943, with more than 700 aircraft bombing the city on each occasion. Smaller USAF raids added to Hamburg's misery with a total of 252 sorties on July 25/26. On the ground, the effect of the raids was horrific. This was the sequence of attacks which generated the firestorm, a monstrous furnace which engulfed 22 square kilometers of the city in temperatures of 1,000 °C and more. Hurricanes of searing air ripped between buildings at speeds up to 200 MPH, incinerating everything in their path. By the time it was all over, perhaps 50,000 people were dead and a million refugees had fled the city. The damage statistics were staggering, and they shook the Nazi leadership to its core — destroyed were 40,385 houses, 275,000 flats, 580 factories, 2,632 shops, 83 banks, 76 public buildings, 277 schools, 24 hospitals, 58 churches, 12 bridges, and a zoo. Hitler's Minister of Armaments, Albert Speer, confessed that: "Hamburg had put the fear of God into me. . . I informed Hitler that a series of attacks of this sort, extended to six more major cities, would bring Germany's armaments production to a total halt."

For all its promise, "Window" proved a two-edged sword. Even during the four RAF raids of the Battle of Hamburg, the German defensive system reacted to it with remarkable resilience. As the Germans fought with some success to free themselves from the morass of "Window," the loss rates on each raid rose to 2.2 percent, 3.6 percent, and finally 4.4 percent. "Window" forced the Germans to rethink their strategy, liberating them from the strait-jacket of the "Kammhuber Line," a rigid defensive system based on the ground-controlled interception of individual bombers. Now they switched first to the use of freelancing day fighters ("Wild Boar") at night, and later to twin-engine night fighters ("Tame Boar") equipped with "Lichtenstein SN2," an airborne radar unaffected by "Window." Vectored into the bomber stream by radio running commentary, the fighters were then left to hunt for themselves. This much more flexible system led to many more interceptions and a steadily rising attrition of the RAF's bomber force.

Even with the bomber force advancing behind a "Window" screen, and with diversionary forces dropping "Window" elsewhere to confuse the defenses, the approach to enemy airspace could still be hazardous, as the crew of a Number 61 Squadron Lancaster found out on their way to Dusseldorf on November 3, 1943. At 21,000 feet, with the Dutch coast in sight, a Messerschmitt 110 hit them hard, its cannon

Flt Lt Bill Reid. Imperial War Museum

shells ripping through the aircraft from end to end, damaging the elevator, both turrets, and the hydraulic system. In the cockpit, the compass was among the instruments out of action and the canopy was shattered. The Scots captain, Flt Lt Bill Reid, was hit in the head and shoulders by shell splinters, and his face was full of Perspex fragments. Pulling his goggles down to protect his eyes from the icy blast, Reid got the stricken Lancaster under control after a loss of 2,000 feet. At first bothered by blood running into his eyes, he soon found that the freezing air coagulated the flow. Since the rest of the crew were unhurt, he decided not to worry them with his problems. Reid said nothing about his injuries and pressed on for Dusseldorf.

Within minutes the Lancaster was struck again, this time by a Focke-Wulf 190, which raked the whole length of the bomber's fuselage with its fire. This attack had more dire effects. The navigator was killed, the wireless operator mortally wounded, and both the flight engineer and Reid were hit. Cannon shells disrupted the oxygen system and further damaged the turrets and hydraulics. After the loss of another 2,000 feet, Reid leveled out and, with his arms wrapped round the control column to hold the nose up and full left rudder to keep straight, he maintained the course for Dusseldorf. "It was only commonsense to keep going," he says. "Turning back against the bomber stream would have been dangerous."

Steering by occasional reference to the Pole Star, Reid reached Dusseldorf about an hour after the second fighter attack and the bombs were delivered on target.

On the way home, the crew survived passage through a heavy flak barrage, the temporary failure of all four engines when a fuel tank emptied unexpectedly, and the drag of bomb doors which could not be closed. However, the strain of holding the aircraft straight and level against the abnormal loads on the controls began to tell on the pilot. Reid lost more blood as his wounds reopened and he went through periods of exhaustion and light-headedness. At last he crossed the English coast and managed to recover sufficiently to land at Shipdam, a USAF base, only to have a much damaged undercarriage collapse on touchdown. On recovery from his injuries, Bill Reid found, much to his expressed astonishment, that he had been awarded the Victoria Cross.

As they closed on the target, bomber crews could become mesmerized by the scene around them. Far from being cocooned in darkness, they sometimes seemed to be swimming in light. Berlin, in particular, could be brilliantly lit — walls of searchlights, hanging flares, multi-colored markers, fires carpeting the ground, flashes from gunfire and exploding bombs, clouds made luminescent by glare — it was a colossal light show without the sound. As one flight engineer put it: "The roar of your engines drowns everything else. It's like running straight into the most gigantic display of soundless fireworks in the world." Some aircraft would be seen transfixed by the stabbing searchlights, encouraging the others to weave and dive to get through. Then would come the breathless tension of the last few moments before bomb release, with the navigator calling time to target, the bomb doors opening, the bomb aimer guiding the closing stages, the call of "Bombs away!", and the sudden lurch upward as the bombs left their shackles. A few moments more until the target photograph was taken, and then it was down and away as the bomber broke for home.

Even over the target in a holocaust of flak, it was never safe to assume that there were no enemy fighters about. Many Luftwaffe

Sergeant Norman Jackson.

pilots ignored the forest of shell bursts to get in among the bombers, silhouetted as they were against the fires below "like flies crawling across a tablecloth." Away from the target, too, the Luftwaffe was relentless in its pursuit of the raiders. Heavily armed night fighters equipped with homing devices and the latest radar hounded the bombers on their homeward flight, often attacking Lancasters where they were most vulnerable, from directly underneath. The absence of a ventral turret now became the Lancaster's Achilles heel, and it was fully exploited by fighters armed with upward-firing cannon, a deadly weapons system known as "Schrage Musik." Sliding beneath an unsuspecting victim, a fighter pilot would carefully line up his guns on the area of the inner wing housing the largest fuel tank and open fire from

point-blank range. Almost invariably, the Lancaster burst into flame and exploded, with the crew never knowing what hit them. In this way, on March 14, 1945, Luftwaffe ace Martin Becker achieved the incredible feat of destroying nine Lancasters in one night.

The Lancaster was sturdily built, but well-directed cannon fire could reduce it to a hopeless pile of wreckage in one short burst. The dramatic change from functioning machine to flaming coffin often inspired responses from crew members which seemed beyond reason. Sergeant Norman Jackson, a flight engineer with Number 106 Squadron, won the Victoria Cross for just such an action. On April 26, 1944, soon after bombing Schweinfurt, Jackson's Lancaster was raked by shells from a Focke-Wulf 190 and the starboard inner engine erupted in flames. The engine fire extinguisher had little effect and the fire rapidly intensified, threatening to spread to the fuel tanks. Jackson did not hesitate. He told the pilot: "I think I can deal with it, Fred. I'll climb out on the wing." Fred Mifflin had his hands full trying to control his damaged aircraft and made no objection, so Jackson put on his parachute and stuffed a fire extinguisher down the front of his battle dress. Climbing onto the navigator's table, he pulled the parachute rip cord and handed the canopy and rigging lines to the navigator and bomb aimer before releasing the upper escape hatch.

As he squeezed himself through the narrow opening, Jackson emerged into a mind-numbingly cold 160 MPH gale. He slid along the side of the fuselage until his boots hit the surface of the wing and then grabbed at the tenuous security of a small air intake in the leading edge. Hanging on with his left hand, he recovered the fire extinguisher with his right and discharged it into the nearest engine intake. He was elated to see that after a few moments the flames began to die down.

Jackson now faced the problem of how to get back inside the fuselage. Before he could make the attempt, however, he felt the wing beneath him lift as the Lancaster rolled sharply to port. The fighter was back. Cannon fire once more tore through the aircraft and Jackson felt the sharp pain of shell splinters entering

his legs and back. The engine fire alongside him burst out afresh and flames swept his body, tearing him off the wing. The tail flashed by and Jackson was left flailing at the end of his rigging lines, several feet behind the tail turret. The doomed bomber was in a twisting fall to earth, but Jackson's colleagues hung on to feed his parachute out of the escape hatch. Suddenly he was falling free, but his trials were not over. He saw that his rigging lines were burning, so he pulled them towards him and smothered them with his bare hands. His fall was rapid because of rips and burns in the parachute canopy, and he hit the ground hard, breaking both ankles. After surviving a night in the open with his terrible injuries, and then enduring a less than friendly reception from the local people, Jackson spent almost a year recuperating slowly in a German hospital, but his burned hands remained a permanent reminder of his extraordinary action.

To the crews, the return flight from the target could be interminable. Evasive routing, devised both to separate inbound and outbound aircraft and keep the Luftwaffe guessing, lengthened the journey, and the invariable westerly headwinds often made for depressingly slow progress over the ground. In those Lancasters carrying wounded and struggling with battle damage, it could seem as though the coast of England would never appear. For some, the cold waters of the North Sea waited. Others lumbered into emergency airfields on the east coast, where ambulance and fire crews were used to handle broken bodies and shattered airframes.

The lucky crews who had come through unscathed to see the winking of their home base beacon began to relax and think about having a beer in the local pub. Nothing was more comforting than to hear the litany of the pre-landing checks and the thump of the undercarriage locking down. A screech of rubber on runway, a muttering of Merlins into dispersal, and then a blessed peace as the fuel was cut off and the engines whistled into silence. They had survived and taken one more step towards the end of their tour.

Special Operations

The Lancaster's exceptional capabili-

Wing Commander
Guy Gibson.

ties made it an ideal aircraft for undertaking operations which demanded the use of special weapons. The most celebrated of these was the raid on German dams in May 1943. An elite unit was formed for this raid, Number 617 Squadron commanded by Wing Commander Guy Gibson, and a cylindrical "bouncing bomb" weighing 9,250 pounds was designed by Dr. Barnes Wallis. Nineteen modified Lancasters took off from RAF Scampton on the evening of May 16, 1943, to attack three of the Ruhr dams (Mohne, Eder, Sorpe) at low-level. Two aircraft had to turn back early. One lost two engines and its bomb in a close encounter with the sea, and the other had a damaging brush with the defenses on the Dutch coast.

The attacks on the dams had to be made from only 60 feet and at exactly 240 MPH. The precise height was judged by the coincidence of two spotlights shining on the surface, and the correct range by lining up two uprights of a homemade bombsight with the towers at each end of the dams. It took four bombs to destroy the Mohne dam and two more to ruin the Eder. The Sorpe, an earth core dam, resisted the one bomb it received. Eight of the 617 Squadron crews were lost — four were shot down by flak, two hit power cables, one ran into a tree, and one was destroyed when the bomb struck the top of the dam wall and exploded under the aircraft.

The raid was immensely destructive to the areas downstream of the dams, but it failed to achieve its object of denying water to the Ruhr industries. The Sorpe's survival ensured that just enough water was retained to keep things going until the other dams were repaired. Nevertheless, from an operational point of view, it was a tour de force, and Gibson was awarded the Victoria Cross for his inspired leadership. Targets impervious to conventional attack had been destroyed in a demonstration of accurate flying and precision bombing unequaled in WWII. It had been shown that the crushing bludgeon of the Lancaster could, when necessary, become a deadly rapier.

Later there were two squadrons equipped with modified Lancasters to take on special operations; 617 was joined by Number IX Squadron. Their weapons were 12,000-

"Grand Slam" bomb weighed 22,400 pounds.

pound "Tallboys" and 22,000-pound "Grand Slams." Between them, they carried out attacks on targets which had been found particularly difficult to destroy, like the Dortmund-Ems canal, the Saumur railway tunnel, U-boat pens, the Heligoland coastal batteries, and the Bielefeld viaduct. On November 30, 1944, the two squadrons sent their Lancasters to attack the battleship *Tirpitz* moored near Tromso in Norway. It was the last of several attempts to sink the ship. Twenty-eight "Tallboys" fell around the *Tirpitz*, with two scoring direct hits and several near misses.

When the raid leader, Wing Commander Willie Tait, landed in Scotland, he was asked if they had got the *Tirpitz*. He thought for a moment and said: "I think so. Gave her a hell of a nudge anyway." Tait's nudge had been more than enough. Within minutes of the attack, the battleship capsized, taking more than 1,000 of her crew to a watery grave.

Lancaster Mark I (Special) of Number 617 Squadron releasing a "Grand Slam."

Promise Realized

By the last year of the war, the Lancaster had become the overpowering weapon that the RAF had sought for so long. Reliable navigation and bombing aids and the development of effective techniques, such as raid management by a master bomber and accurate marking, meant that the Lancaster could find and hit (or at least seriously "nudge") almost any target in almost any weather, day or night. Used in large numbers, Lancasters were awesomely destructive, as was made all too terrifyingly apparent at Dresden on February 13, 1945, when 796 Lancasters dropped more than 2,600 tons of high explosive and incendiaries and obliterated the center of the city. Ten days later, the same treatment was meted out to the city of Pforzheim, when 367 Lancasters destroyed 83 percent of the built-up area.

Bombers had begun to become markedly safer places to be after the D-Day invasion. The German early warning line was being pushed back and Luftwaffe airfields were coming within easy reach of strafing Allied fighters. Germany's oil supply was dwindling and the Luftwaffe could no longer react to every threat. In January 1944, Bomber Command had lost more than 300 four-engine aircraft while flying a little more than 6,200 sorties. By October, the losses were down to 75 aircraft in nearly 10,200 sorties. (It is a revealing comment on the scale of operations in the latter stages of WWII that the loss of 75 four-engine aircraft in one month, the equivalent of almost a squadron per week, could be regarded as relatively insignificant.) Nineteen forty-five saw the fighter arm of the Luftwaffe being progressively destroyed in combat with the USAF, both in the air and on the ground. This enabled the RAF's bombers to return to daylight operation, and the closing months of the war saw Lancasters roaming over Germany to attack with near impunity targets which had cost Bomber Command dearly in earlier years. A force of 750 Lancasters was at the core of more than 1,000 aircraft sent on raids against Essen and Dortmund in March 1945. In both places, nearly 5,000 tons of bombs produced destruction so complete that the cities were effectively paralyzed. Two Lancasters were lost over Dortmund and three over Essen.

The last great bomber assault on a German target came on April 25, 1945. In an attack which was symbolic of Allied war aims, 359 Lancasters were sent to Berchtesgaden to strike at Hitler's "Eagle's Nest" and the nearby SS barracks. Next day, the Lancaster force shed its martial role for good and began flying into Europe to collect recently liberated prisoners of war. In the days which followed, some 75,000 men were taken back to the UK and the promise of peace. In Operation Manna, between April 29 and May 7, 1945, Lancasters also flew 2,835 sorties to drop 6,000 tons of food to the starving Dutch population.

The Cost

The battles were over and it was time to count the cost. For Bomber Command as a whole, it had been severe. About 125,000 men served with the Command as aircrew on operations against Germany between 1939 and 1945. Of those, 55,500 died, 85 percent of them during operations; 8,403 were wounded; and a further 9,838 were taken prisoner, many of whom were also wounded. The casualty list therefore totals 73,741, or nearly 60 percent of all those involved. Among the combatants of all services on both sides, only the German U-boat service proved more lethal to its practitioners.

The statistics on crew survival during the hardest days of 1943/44, when Sir Arthur Harris was pounding away at Berlin, make especially somber reading. Of every 100 aircrew entering a Bomber Command operational training unit at that time, it was calculated that 51 would be killed on operations, and another 9 in crashes. Three would be injured badly enough to be removed from aircrew status, and 12 would survive the destruction of their aircraft to be taken prisoner. It was thought that one would both survive being shot down and evade capture. That left less than a quarter of the total who could expect to complete a tour of operations unscathed.

Bomber Command launched a total of 389,809 operational sorties in the course of the air offensive against Germany. These were flown on over 71 percent of the nights and 52 percent of the days between September 1939 and June 1945. Although not in combat until 1942, the Lancaster bore the brunt of the battle, flying 156,192 sorties. It was the aircraft which led the way in the Bomber Command Battles of the Ruhr, Hamburg, and Berlin, in RAF bomber operations supporting D-Day and the Battle of Normandy, and in Bomber Command's final assault on Germany. (In second place was the Halifax with a total of 82,773 sorties.) Three thousand four hundred thirty-one Lancs were lost, and a further 246

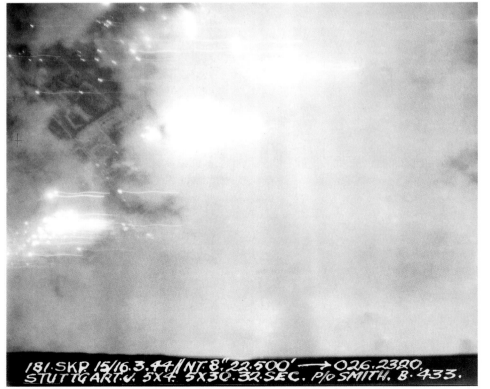

RAF strike photograph from a raid over Stuttgart, March 15/16, 1944, taken from 22, 500 feet at 11:20 P.M.

Lancaster Mark III of Number 103 Squadron preparing for take-off, March 1943.

were listed as having "crashed in the United Kingdom while on operational flights," for a combined loss rate of 2.36 percent. The rates for the Halifax and Stirling were 2.52 percent and 3.71 percent respectively, but it should be remembered that for much of the war the Lancaster was preferred to these types for the more difficult targets. When all three were involved, for example in raids against Berlin in 1943, the difference between the types was marked — Lancaster 5.4 percent, Halifax 8.8 percent, Stirling 12.9 percent. In Bomber Command's worst loss of the war, 95 aircraft against Nuremburg on March 30, 1944, when three-quarters of the force of nearly 800 aircraft were Lancasters, the difference was still evident — Lancaster 11.2 percent, Halifax 14.5 percent.

Almost half the total tonnage of bombs dropped by Bomber Command in five and a half years of war was dropped in the last nine months. In Germany, the progressive destruction of the cities was dramatic evidence that the bomber offensive was visiting a fearful retribution on the German people. When peace came, there were many who were only too ready to suggest that such destruction had been willful and to point out that strategic bombing had not lived up to the promise of air power theorists that the war could be won by air assault alone.

These opinions paid little heed to the long years when RAF Bomber Command was the only offensive instrument available for striking at a rampant Germany. For the British people in their darkest days it was the bomber aircrew who kept the offensive flame burning and lit the way to eventual victory. After the war, Albert Speer noted that the bomber offensive "opened a second front long before the Allied invasion," and he drew attention to the enormous effort expended in defending against the bombers: ". . . thousands of guns, tremendous quantities of ammunition, hundreds of thousands of soldiers." There were also squadrons of fighters and the whole defensive structure supported by large elements of German industry and the transportation system. These resources could have been deployed elsewhere in the absence of a bomber offensive.

The bomber crews paid a terrible price for their achievement, and that was never formally recognized. Postwar political sensitivity over the bombing offensive led to a refusal to issue a special campaign medal to those who had taken part. There were, of course, many gallantry medals for individual performances, although even these could only be representative of the extraordinary levels of courage and determination demonstrated by hundreds of aircrew on every raid. Among the awards to

bomber aircrew were 19 Victoria Crosses, and ten of these went to members of Lancaster crews.* But for the spirit and sacrifice of such men and their colleagues, the war would have been an even longer and bloodier conflict.

---

*Lancaster VCs

See text for John Nettleton (44 Sqn), Guy Gibson (617 Sqn), Bill Reid (61 Sqn), Norman Jackson (106 Sqn). Others: Andrew Mynarski (419 Sqn), Ian Bazalgette (635 Sqn), Robert Palmer (109 Sqn), George Thompson (IX Sqn), Edwin Swales (582 Sqn), Leonard Cheshire (617 Sqn, for operations with Lancasters and Mosquitos).

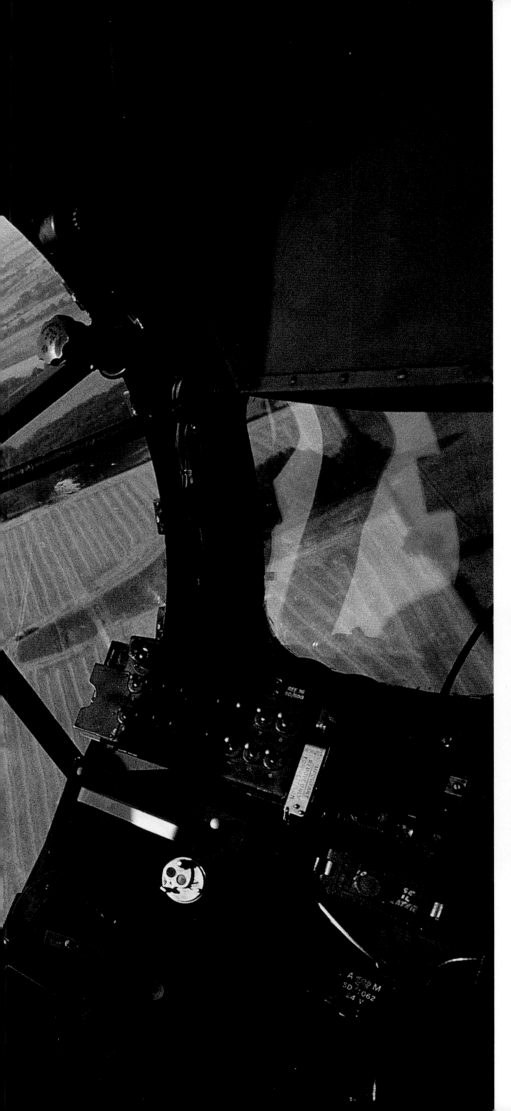

Previous page: The nose section of the Lancaster, this one in the colors of a famous IX Squadron aircraft, Johnny Walker, *which completed 106 operational sorties. Above the open bomb bay doors, the greenhouse canopy over the cockpit. Forward is the bomb aimer/nose gunner position.*

A   Looking to the twelve o'clock position, the bomb aimer's view, through the Perspex nose of the bomber. Because of the powered turret above the bombsight, the crewman had to lie on his stomach on the cushion at bottom to reach his sight. To the right is the panel he used to control the bomb drop. The bomb aimer had double duties, as he had to man the turret when not occupied with the task of placing bombs on the target. Lancaster missions were often flown at low level.

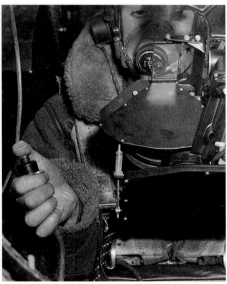

Imperial War Museum

(In above and subsequent diagrams, gray area denotes aircraft section depicted in photographs.)

A   The bomb aimer over the bombsight; in his right hand is the bomb release button. Since the Perspex nose cone of the Lancaster was not optically corrected, the round insert in the cone is flat optical glass, giving the bomb aimer the ability to find his target and checkpoints without the distraction of a blurred view. Other distractions would be enemy flak, fighters, and searchlights, as well as other Lancasters. Night missions were not flown in formation; often the bomber would fly through the prop wash of another plane, without either of them seeing each other.

B   The bomb aimer's control panel; the switches on top are the 16 selection switches for the bombload. The circular control at bottom is an intervalometer, which can automatically release the bombload in a programmed pattern, based on the speed of the bomber and the desired pattern of bomb delivery. The bombs could be dropped in a "stick" designed to spread the bombs over a target or salvoed to drop all at once.

C   The bomb aimer's stopwatch, in the clip on the right side of the fuselage. The control at lower right is the selector to determine the order of dropping, an important factor in maintaining the balance of the bomber, as the bomb bay is 33 feet long. An uncontrolled release could make the airplane unflyable.

B

C

A   *The powered nose turret, over the nose cone. Twin .303-caliber machine guns, slightly elevated, point directly forward. Head-on attacks were not a common occurrence in night operations. In addition to his job as bomb aimer, forward defense of the Lancaster was also the duty of the crewman in the nose. Another task was to release the foil strips of "Window" at predetermined intervals in the mission. These clouds of foil dropped by Lancasters on a mission served to confuse German radar.*

B   *The nose turret gunner's view from behind the gunsight; the turret structure surrounds him.*

C   *Looking forward to the twelve o'clock position over the right-side machine gun; the second gun barrel is visible at left.*

Collection of Kurt Weidner

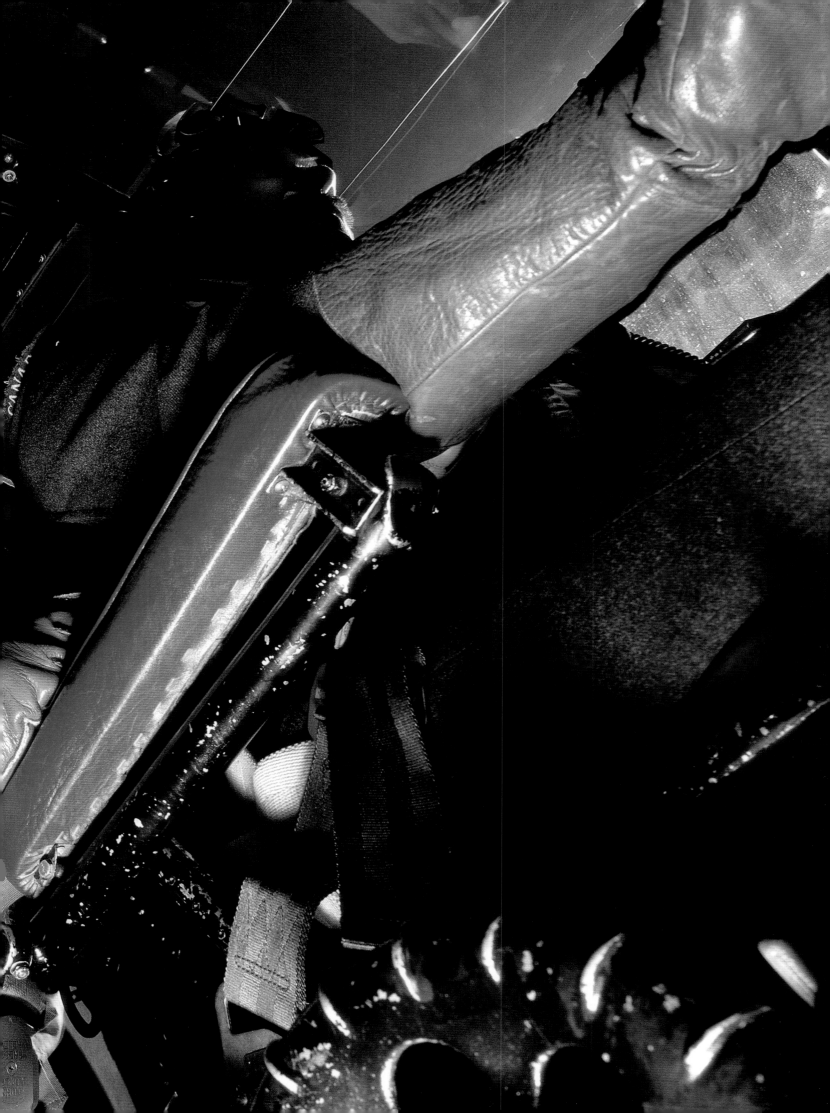

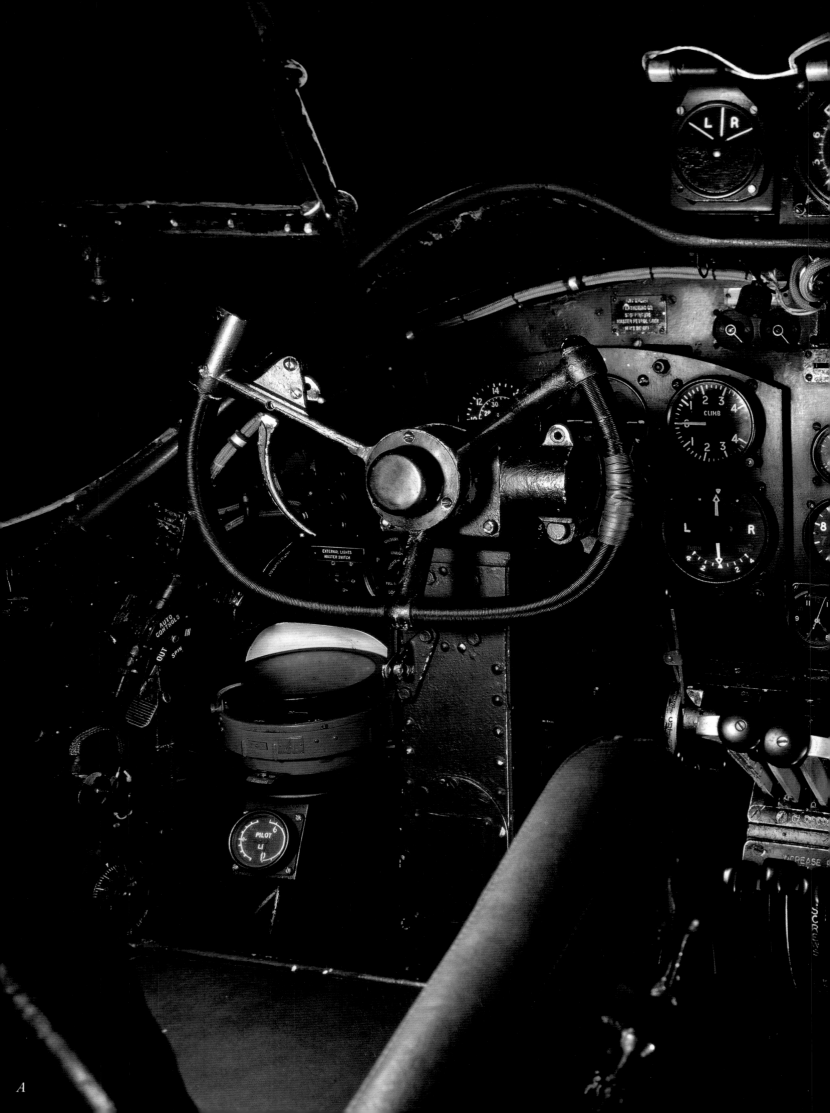

Previous page: The cockpit crew of three; at top right is the pilot. RAF bombers were flown as single-pilot airplanes, unlike their American counterparts, which had two pilots. Center is the flight engineer, who monitored the performance of the Rolls-Royce Merlin engines and other systems. He could fly the bomber if the pilot was wounded or killed. Bottom left is the navigator, who was responsible for guiding the bomber through night skies to a distant target at a specific time. He was also tasked with the job of operating the electronic countermeasures that became increasingly sophisticated as the war progressed.

A	The cockpit instrument panel of the Lancaster. The single pilot seat and control column are at left. Just below the control yoke is the large magnetic compass, floating in a pool of oil. Directly in front of the yoke are the flight instruments, airspeed, altimeter, rate of climb, and turn indicator. Bottom center are the throttle controls and propeller controls. The right side of the panel contains the engine instruments. The red buttons at bottom right are to feather the propellers. Should an engine be damaged, the propeller's pitch is turned knife edge to the airflow over the wings to reduce the amount of drag. Below is the crawl way that leads to the nose of the plane.

A   RAF flight crews were often made up of members from several nations of the Commonwealth or from the USA. A typical bomber crew could well have individuals from Canada, New Zealand, and Australia in addition to those from Britain. The pilot would at times have to perform some dramatic aerobatics as evasive maneuvers. The Lancaster was a remarkably agile airplane considering its size and weight. The "corkscrew" was a particularly effective maneuver either to the right or left, to throw off the aim of an attacking fighter. Evasive maneuvering was often directed by a gunner in one of the turrets in the back of the plane.

B   The exterior antennae for the "Rebecca" blind landing system.

A

C

A   The pilot's control yoke; on the crossbar is the push-to-talk switch for communicating with the crew over the intercom or to talk on the radio.

B   The back of the pilot's seat is 1/4" steel armor plate. The Lancaster carried very little other armor protection.

C   Looking forward from the wireless operator's position to the cockpit. The panel on the right is the flight engineer's station; just ahead of that is a folded-down jump seat. Beyond that is the passageway into the nose.

D   The pilot's engine controls— throttle, fuel mixture, and propeller pitch.

Next page: Looking to the three o'clock position from the flight engineer's station; engines #3 and #4 and the right wing.

B

D

The flight engineer's control panel. Following orders from the pilot, the engineer monitored the engines, fuel use, and other mechanical operations of the bomber during a mission. The red knobs at center left are the fuel tank selectors, the yellow gauges at top right are for monitoring oil temperature, the gauges just below indicate the coolant temperature. Below those are gauges that show the engineer the amounts of fuel remaining in the individual tanks.

The engineer at his station; behind him is the navigator. The engineer would keep the pilot informed as to the available options if the bomber was damaged in combat. All crewmen kept a sharp eye out for enemy fighters; many Lancasters were shot down when a mission was nearly over. German intruders would follow the bombers back to base and attack them after the crew felt they were safe over home territory.

A   The navigator's station, directly behind the pilot's seat. At top right are flight instruments that gave the navigator altitude and compass headings. At center is the "Gee" box, one of the electronic navigational tools developed by the British to facilitate effective bombing and navigating over hostile territory at night. The navigator in the Lancaster was often isolated from the rest of the crew, his position curtained off to allow him to work with a light on. Any light showing from the blacked-out bomber in night skies could be fatal, as the German night fighters were always present.

Imperial War Museum

40

B

B   Another valuable electronic weapon was the H2S air-to-ground radar. This system enabled a bomber crew to find the target and bomb through overcast. It was most effective, however, when used against targets that had distinctive geographic features, such as a coastline or the mouth of a waterway, that could be easily picked out on a small radar screen. These screens would be even more difficult to read if the bomber was under attack and being put through evasive maneuvers.

C   Looking directly aft along the top of the fuselage, from the navigator's station, towards the Fraser-Nash mid-upper turret.

C

A

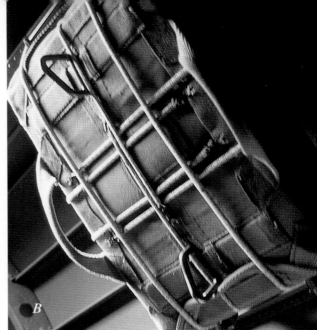

A The wireless operator's station. This crewman's duties were to maintain contact with the Bomber Command channels for any alterations in the mission once they had taken off, to make regular position reports, and to report on the results of the mission after the bombs had been dropped. After 1942, wireless operators were cross trained as gunners, with a designation of "WAG," for wireless operator air-gunner.

B A standard RAF chest-type parachute, stored in the rack along the side of the fuselage, just above and to the right of the wireless operator's seat.

C The wireless operator's table, with engine #2 out the window.

A   *Inside the massive Lancaster bomb bay. The bay extends for 33 feet, almost half the length of the fuselage. Bombloads could be widely varied to contain high explosives, incendiaries, or combinations of both. During the war the RAF developed huge high explosive weapons. A commonly used bomb was the "Cookie," a 4,000-pound high explosive that was sometimes combined with other bombs to create a more devastating attack. Also used in specially modified Lancasters were the "Tallboy," a 12,000-pound bomb, and the "Grand Slam," or earthquake bomb, that weighed a staggering 22,000 pounds. Designed with offset fins to make them spin when released, they reached supersonic speeds as they fell to earth. They were meant to bury themselves 100 feet or more into the earth before detonating, thus creating an earthquake effect.*

B   *To the rear of the bomb bay is the H2S dome containing the radar antennae.*

B

A   *Beyond the bomb bay, the Fraser-Nash mid-upper turret. This turret was an important part of the bomber defense, providing the gunner with an unobstructed view from the top of the plane in all directions.*

B   *Looking through the turret structure, forward to the eleven o'clock position. Engines #1 and #2 and the left wing are visible.*

Next page: Looking to the six o'clock position, the right vertical stabilizer and elevator.

Collection of Kurt Weidner

Previous page: The rear turret, the mid-upper turret, and the broad shoulder wing of the Lancaster. The wing spans 102 feet; the split flaps are visible along the bottom of the wing's trailing edge.

A   The rear turret of the Lancaster carried four .303-caliber machine guns. Later versions were mounted with heavier .50-caliber machine guns, considered to be more effective against the German fighters.

B   Belts of the .303-caliber ammunition leading into the breeches of two of the guns in the rear turret, with the barrels visible in the background.

C   Looking across the breeches of the rear turret machine guns.

Next page: Looking to the six o'clock position from the rear turret, all four guns are visible. From here the gunner could inform the pilot of any incoming attacks and also the results of the bombing. Rear gunners would often remove or cut out the center panel of the Perspex turret to give them an unobstructed view out into the night sky. An approaching night fighter could be very difficult to see.

B

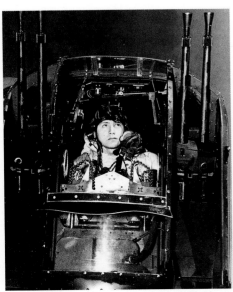

Imperial War Museum

C

A

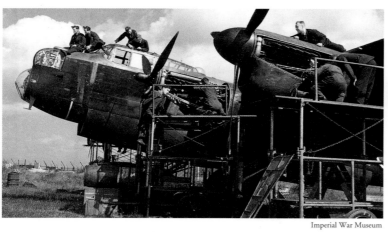

Imperial War Museum

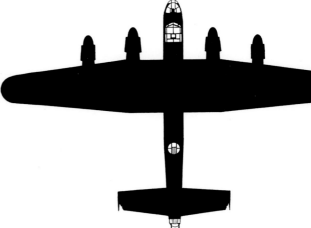

56

A The Lancaster was powered by four Rolls-Royce Merlin engines. These reliable power plants were also used in the Spitfire, Hurricane, and P-51 Mustang. These engines developed 1,175 horsepower each. The relatively light weight of the Lancaster, 37,000 pounds empty and 60-65,000 pounds fully loaded, combined with the surplus of available power that four of these engines provided, gave the RAF a very flexible weapon that could fill many roles.

B Engine #3, on the right wing. Beyond the nose of the bomber is a typical RAF air base support building.

C The inboard engines and nacelles on the Lancaster carried the massive main landing gear. The bomber's 20-foot ground clearance allowed for the modification of some aircraft to carry the enormous high explosive weapons used by the RAF during the war.

During engine start a ground crewman was required to stand on the main wheel and prime the engines with a hand pump, squirting raw fuel into the engines until they started.

Collection of Kurt Weidner

A typical RAF bomber crew, standing at the main entry door. This door was a dangerous place to get out of a disabled bomber at night over enemy territory. Crewmen who bailed out here would often strike the stabilizer that is so close to the door. The almost inevitable result would be death.

This Canadian Mark X Lancaster carries a Martin upper turret, identical to the upper turret in the B-24 Liberator. This turret is armed with two .50-caliber machine guns.

Imperial War Museum

Collection of Kurt Weidner

59

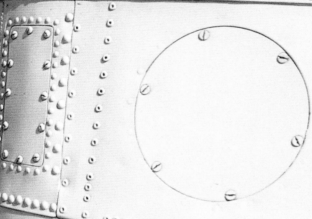

A

A   In the foreground, the left vertical stabilizer. Beyond is the center fuselage and open bomb bay doors. Above the RAF roundel and call letters is the mid-upper turret.

B   With Rolls-Royce Merlin engines running, a Lancaster warms up.

C   Engines #1 and #2; beneath are the radiators for the liquid-cooled power plants.

D   A Lancaster taxis out to the active runway.

Next page: Merlin engines at full power, the Lancaster roars into the air.

Collection of Kurt Weidner

Acknowledgments

This book would not have been possible without the help and cooperation of the following people and organizations. We owe them our thanks.

Lancaster, *Just Jane*

Fred and Harold Panton of The East Kirkby Aviation Heritage Center, East Kirkby, Lincolnshire, UK. These brothers have preserved a true gem, not only the Lancaster, but also an airfield from which these bombers left on their missions. Their brother was shot down during a Bomber Command raid during World War II, and this is a memorial to him and all the others who did not return from the war. Ron Emeny, a veteran of the Lancaster force who provided insight into the perils of the job, and Catherine East for wonderful hospitality.

Lancaster, PA474, *City of Lincoln*

This Lancaster is operated by the Battle of Britain Memorial Flight, Royal Air Force, and based at RAF Coningsby, Lincolnshire, commanded by Squadron Leader Rick Groombridge, pilot Flight Lieutenant Mike Chatterton. This is the last Lancaster owned and operated by the RAF, and is one of two still flying. The BBMF continues to fly the airplanes of World War II. In addition to the Lanc, they also operate several Spitfires, one of the few remaining Hurricanes, and a Douglas Dakota. Flying Officer Sue Gardner was very helpful and made it possible to get the photography accomplished in the short time available.

Lancaster, Mynarski Memorial

Owned and operated by the Canadian Warplane Heritage Museum, Mt. Hope, Ontario. This is the other Lancaster still flying in the world. Bill Randall, Gil Hunt, and his crew deserve our thanks. Jim Buckel, Randy Straughan, and Wilf Riddle were kind enough to suit up and help provide "crewmen" for the photography.

Kurt Weidner has provided invaluable help and assistance in the production of this book. Kurt's knowledge of the subject and his personal collection of authentic artifacts added the "little" things that make these books come to life.

Jim O'Neill, another collector and expert, who made the photographs in this book possible.

Bruce Zigler and Tom Horton, who drove all night to come to the rescue when I needed the help and who provided invaluable knowledge and assistance for the photography in Canada.

My children, Nate, Brigitta, and Joe, who understand when Dad "takes off" to chase airplanes.

Kelly Miller, for unquestioning support.

Paul Perkins, my lifelong friend.

Ross Howell and Howell Press, Elinor Howell, and Kate Neale.

I would also like to thank Tom Kosicki, Troy Mulvaine, Hugh Daly, Dave Barry, Dave Ireland, Bart Reames, David Hake, Rob Barnes.

Eric and Joan Johnson, of "The Blue Bell," a pub outside Coningsby, Lincolnshire, where we found wonderful hospitality, good food, and smooth ale. Eric introduced us to the Panton brothers and made it possible to unwind after long days of work.

Ron Dick and his wife Paul; without their help, there would be no book. I was able to see England with a "guide" who has no equal. Ron has become a close friend and colleague, and I value his friendship and opinion.

Technical Notes

The original photography in this book was all done with the intent to as faithfully as possible remove the clues of the present day and try to look back through a window opened by the owners and operators of these aircraft, a window into the 1940s when formations of these airplanes flew over the European continent during World War II.

I used a variety of cameras and equipment to complete this project: a Wista 4x5 Field View camera with a 150mm Caltar II lens and a 90mm Nikkor lens; a Mamiya RB67 with 50mm, 90mm, and 180mm lenses; and a Nikon F3 with a motor drive and a garden variety of Nikkor lenses.

All the photographs were shot as transparencies to make the best possible color separations.

The 4x5 and 6x7 photos were all shot on Kodak Ektachrome Daylight film. The 35mm photos were taken with Ektachrome as well as Kodachrome 200.

The concept, design, and the photographs are done by Dan Patterson, 6825 Peters Pike, Dayton, Ohio 45414.